PRAISE FOR *BROKEN GIFTS*

Broken Gifts is a heartfelt description of what a mother and the family go through with a family member with mental health issues. The book offers the reader the opportunity to see into the thoughts and feelings of someone struggling with mental health and severe medical issues through poems and journals of the writer's son, Aaron. It also provides an opportunity to bring awareness of the lack of mental health services available for people in need and the connection between religion, family, and people that are challenged with mental health symptoms.

—Jason Waldmeier
Licensed Specialist Clinical Social Worker

I just finished reading your manuscript. I am blessed and inspired by your and Aaron's special gift of communicating through the written word. I am confident that anyone who reads your family's story will also be inspired by your confidence and faithfulness to and in God's Word. It is the way you survived, and it will give hope to all who read *Broken Gifts*. Your statement, "God alone is the solution to every imaginable dilemma we will ever encounter," is the prayer I pray for all who read *Broken Gifts*.

—Sue Ellen Ferguson
Director of Recovery Ministries
Council Road Baptist Church
Bethany, Oklahoma

Broken Gifts is a touching, unflinchingly honest, and highly readable book that takes a compassionate look at the impact of mental illness on a family who had done "all the right things" and yet still faces the anguish and heartbreak of watching a beloved child slide into a pit of unreasoning rage, reckless rebellion, and profound depression. It captures the oppressive weight of the feeling that you have failed, but you don't know how or when or why, and you have no idea how to fix things. For the church community, it provides a warning against the judgment that is so easy to arise in our simplistic criticisms when we see the struggling child or family in our midst. And through it all, this mother and family were sustained by the amazing grace of the lord Jesus Christ that enabled them to "accept, embrace, and to love those gifts that are broken."

—Diana Waters, PhD
Clinical Psychologist

*Broken Gifts i*s the story of Aaron. Through his writings, we understand the anguish and heartbreak he experienced, and his ability to move beyond mental illness and it's devastating effects to a sense of hope and fulfillment. *Broken Gifts* also includes Jill's journey of heartbreak and to hope.

—Cara Martin Raffety LCSW
Founding Director of Future & Hope Outreach

The *Broken Gift* is a mother's tribute to her son Aaron, whose life ended too early, and to her family. Aaron was an extremely talented and deeply unsettled person who journaled his search for the meaning of life, questions about his relationship with God, and observed his struggles from within. The book is an honest recollection of the mother's, the son's and the family's difficult times and triumphs, and it is an invitation to us to start opening up and sharing our struggles with each other knowing that we are not alone.

—Svetlana Van Hooser, MA, LPC

BROKEN GIFTS

JILL SMOOT

BROKEN GIFTS

UNWRAPPING THE THOUGHTS OF A WOUNDED MIND

TATE PUBLISHING
AND ENTERPRISES, LLC

Broken Gifts
Copyright © 2015 by Jill Smoot. All rights reserved.

No part of this publication may be reproduced, stored in a retrieval system or transmitted in any way by any means, electronic, mechanical, photocopy, recording or otherwise without the prior permission of the author except as provided by USA copyright law.

Scripture quotations marked (ESV) are from *The Holy Bible, English Standard Version*®, copyright © 2001 by Crossway Bibles, a publishing ministry of Good News Publishers. Used by permission. All rights reserved.

Scripture quotations marked (NASB) are taken from the *New American Standard Bible*®, Copyright © 1960, 1962, 1963, 1968, 1971, 1972, 1973, 1975, 1977, 1995 by The Lockman Foundation. Used by permission.

Scripture quotations marked (NIV) are taken from the *Holy Bible, New International Version*®, NIV®. Copyright © 1973, 1978, 1984 by Biblica, Inc.™ Used by permission of Zondervan. All rights reserved worldwide. www.zondervan.com

Scripture quotations marked (NLT) are taken from the *Holy Bible, New Living Translation*, copyright © 1996. Used by permission of Tyndale House Publishers, Inc., Wheaton, Illinois 60189. All rights reserved.

The opinions expressed by the author are not necessarily those of Tate Publishing, LLC.

Published by Tate Publishing & Enterprises, LLC
127 E. Trade Center Terrace | Mustang, Oklahoma 73064 USA
1.888.361.9473 | www.tatepublishing.com

Tate Publishing is committed to excellence in the publishing industry. The company reflects the philosophy established by the founders, based on Psalm 68:11,
"*The Lord gave the word and great was the company of those who published it.*"

Book design copyright © 2015 by Tate Publishing, LLC. All rights reserved.
Cover design by Rtor Maghuyop
Interior design by Jake Muelle

Published in the United States of America
ISBN: 978-1-63418-169-3
1. Family & Relationships / Children with Special Needs
2. Self-Help / Mood Disorders/ Bipolar Disorder
15.01.29

In memory of our deeply loved son Aaron

Acknowledgments

After the death of our son, when the numbing effect of grief gives way to reality, I began to allow myself to go through Aaron's journals, notebooks, and personal writings. At first it was too painful. As I began to read about his inner struggles, I would have to back off, but then I found quite surprising that even though it hurt to read about all this, it was also healing.

I found also that it helped me gain insight into our son's world and perhaps, into the minds of others like him. The thought came to me that this should be shared, and it startled me to think that. The thought of baring my heart and the difficult times we went through seemed too raw, and was God really speaking to me to do this? Could all the suffering be used in such a way to somehow touch another life? Only the Lord knows how inadequate I felt. What were my qualifications? Grief? Sorrow? Weakness?

So without telling anyone at first, I began crying my way through writing this book, trying to be objective and writing as God gave me thoughts in amazing ways. I felt compelled to keep on, whether it became a book or not. My desire was that God be glorified. So I give thanks to my dearest friend, my greatest treasure, the Lord Jesus Christ, for the completion of what He began.

I would also like to express thanks to those of you who have gifted me with your encouragement, your interest, and your prayers as the book began reality.

To my dear husband, Dwight, who tackled the job of teaching me how to find my way on the laptop, helping me learn skills unknown to me, and for my daughter Rachel, for also sharing her computer know-how, and for son Jeremy who contributed long distance help also. Thank you all so much.

For our children, Adam, Jeremy, Anna, and Rachel, and their precious spouses, Brennan, Tiffany, Sean, and their children, Whitney, Tyler, Connor, Cooper, Reagan, and Cole, you all lived through the painful times as well.

To my listening friends, always willing to hear, at times, my moans and groans. Your belief in the message of this book gave me strength to persevere. Thank you Beverly Flickner, Svetlana Van Hooser, Nancy Kolokotrones, and Verda Riley.

To my church family at Sunnyside and those who prayed with me through some rough places. Thank you for your encouragement for asking how the book was coming along and just for being there for me.

Special thanks to those of you who read the manuscript and wrote endorsements. Some of you I have not had the privilege of meeting yet. Thank you so much for your kindness Sue Ellen Ferguson, Cara Martin Raffety, Jason Waldemeier, and Diana Waters.

I am thankful to Tate Publishing for the awesome opportunity given to me in publishing this book. Thank you to all those involved in every aspect of producing this book—Angela Chris Avancena, Rtor Maghuyop, Jake Muelle, Juan Carlo Villarba, Geoffrey Honculada, and Joseph Villa.

For everything and in everything, may Jesus Christ be praised.

I will never forget this awful time, as I grieve over my loss,
yet I still dare to hope when I remember this; The unfailing
love of the Lord never ends! By his mercies we have been
kept from complete destruction. Great is his faithfulness.
—Lamentations 3:20–23 (NLT)

God, would You give me a gift that's broken,
with fragments piercing sharp?
And when I try to mend it? Fix it?
It shatters, breaks apart.
Why, Giver of all that's good,
do Your gifts come sometimes torn?
And joy lies hidden in sorrow,
and I'm blinded by the thorn.
Oh, God, open these tearstained eyes,
enabling me to see, that giving thanks for broken gifts
is transforming grace to me.

Contents

Preface		17
Chapter 1:	The Gift of a Son	19
Chapter 2:	The Gift That Costs	23
Chapter 3:	The Gift of Peace	25
Chapter 4:	The Gift of Closure	29
Chapter 5:	The Gift of Mercy	33
Chapter 6:	The Gift of a Creative Mind	35
Chapter 7:	The Gift of Seeking Truth	39
Chapter 8:	The Gift of Prayer	43
Chapter 9:	The Gift of Counting It Joy	45
Chapter 10:	The Gift of Endurance	49
Chapter 11:	The Gift of Loneliness	53
Chapter 12:	The Gift of Darkness	57
Chapter 13:	The Gift of Comfort	61
Chapter 14:	The Gift of Weakness	65
Chapter 15:	The Gift of Hope	69
Chapter 16:	The Gift of Refining	73
Chapter 17:	The Gift of Solace	77
Chapter 18:	The Gift of Not Giving Up	81
Chapter 19:	The Gift of Surrender	85
Chapter 20:	The Gift of Acceptance	89
Chapter 21:	The Gift of Gratefulness	93

Chapter 22: The Gift of Compassion 97
Chapter 23: The Gift of Guidance. 101
Chapter 24: The Gift of Grace 105
Chapter 25: The Priceless Gift. 111
Postscript 113
Notes 115

Preface

After our son's untimely death on August 18, 2011, we discovered a vast amount of his writings.

In this collection were poems, stories, plays, letters, and personal journals.

What is significant about this, besides the value they have been for us, is they represent a window into the mind and heart of one who was able to document his journey and struggle with mental issues.

Why is that important today? Perhaps because the profile of those like our son is seen only through outward behavior, and often, others fail to see the real person. They fail to see that they are people who are highly talented but cannot seem to fit into mainstream society. So many times, they are perceived as simply lacking willpower or inner resolve to get it all together.

Why and how they come to be mentally unstable is not for me to understand or define. But what I feel is needed is to see the suffering and inner struggle they deal with and understand that. But how is this possible? We who may occasionally succumb to a bout of depression now and then do manage to get over it. Our minds run on a different track than do those who cannot move on but live daily, yearly, with a mind-set unknown to us.

As much as I longed to help our son, to try to understand him all those years, I never quite did. But now, as I have read his private words, I have new understanding not just for our son, but for those like him.

Recorded in Aaron's writings are his feelings, longings, failures, and battles. On paper, he was able to pour out all his hurt. Perhaps his pain portrays the hearts of those who feel as he did but are not gifted in writing.

For those who will read of our story and will journey with our family as we sometimes crawled through the maze of bewilderment and disappointment, I pray it will prove helpful, especially to those going through similar situations. For those who cannot identify, I pray they will gain insights from our struggle.

I, too, faced battles in those difficult days, and I pray that those who read of these will not come away with sadness but of how our God and Savior, Jesus Christ, gives us what is needed one step at a time—even in our times of "brokenness," God is there giving us gifts. Yet we can fail to "see" them, as we look through the lens of pain. We can be blind to the blessings. Suffering will always exist, at least in this life. But can there not be "hidden treasures" in the darkness? May God impart to us the ability to be looking always in each thorn for the rose hidden within?

Whether strength, wisdom, endurance, or, most of all, His grace. And with that amazing grace, we are enabled to accept, embrace, and to love those gifts that are broken.

1

THE GIFT OF A SON

"Behold, children are a gift of the Lord..."
—Psalm 127:3 (NIV)

God gave us a gift. It was a son, a firstborn boy. In fear and trembling, we held him in our arms to be loved and nurtured, to laugh and to cry with. Amazing. And the gift from God grew, gave joy, but also pain we could not comprehend. Why would this gift become broken? This is my story and perhaps the story for all who love those who are mentally unstable.

Like a bird created to fly, to soar, but instead limps through life with a hurt wing, not understanding nor being understood. We, the onlookers, long for their healing. We try to bind up the brokenness, and we come to understand that God's purpose in it all along was not so much to have answers to our searching, but to receive from His Hand "the fellowship of His sufferings" (Philippians 3:10, NASB).

As you will see, I did not learn this quickly, or easily. Just as when I was a child, I was always on the lookout for what I could "fix," whether a bird, a turtle, or a sick bunny. Carrying it over into adult life—the belief that all questions had answers and were fixable—got in the way of God in my life.

Like uniquely crafted snowflakes, no two are alike. Yet collectively they are the same. We, individually created beings, also share with one another common bonds of grief and suffering. We gain insight and strength from each other's journey through the dark places. And by God's grace, we can learn to open our hands to receive whatever gift God gives, even though painful.

I am not here to write about the cause of mental illness, only its effects. This is for the ones who love those who are affected and have to cope with all the heartache that is a part of it.

In today's church body, there exists a myriad of ministries directed toward those who need help—the single parent, bereaved widow, the poor and needy. The list goes on. Yet perhaps the last frontier to recognize and offer support is to those who have to live with—and deal with—a loved one whose mind is not functioning normally

Granted the body of Christ is not made up of psychologists, but we are called to come alongside those who are suffering. What is worse than dealing with someone who looks normal, yet brings so much suffering into the lives of others?

A medical diagnosis of a known disease warrants sympathy and compassion. Yet how does one share that their son is mentally unstable and they need help? Of course they should do this, but the responses that they may receive can cause them to retreat into a silent shell. Why is this?

Could it be in our "Christian" thought process, we think that, somehow, if we did all the "spiritually correct" things, then those we love would never be involved in any type of addiction, much less any form of mental confusion?

I have to honestly ask myself, did I believe this? Even knowing that only God could make a true home, knowing that families weren't perfect, and knowing that only through Christ was anything of lasting value. Yet, did I think that because we were Christians, while we would have struggles, we were safe?

One woman I know of shared with her Sunday school teacher and her class that she was suffering from depression. The teacher's response was to tell her in front of the class that she needed to just pray more. What embarrassment, and what was the message? Christians just need to pray more, as if she were one deficient in faith.

Randy Alcorn, in his book *If God Is Good*, wrote of a time of depression in his life. "When I wrote about what I was learning from the depression, someone brought me a 'prophetic word' that I was depressed because I wasn't trusting God. Ironically, I had come to trust God deeper in the midst of the depression than I had before it."[1]

For those who have never experienced any situation that has to do with this subject, I say this is most of all for you. Read and allow yourself to walk down some of these paths so when you do meet someone who is there, you will understand.

What happens in the lives of those who are in close contact with someone in mental trauma? I say trauma because the ones who love them are often the ones who are victimized. The stress of living with someone who could explode into rage or weep uncontrollably is a life of living on a thin line.

What is the strength, the power, the ability to get through perhaps a lifetime of this demanding way of life?

Each person has a different story, yet there is a thread linking each one together. The thread is Jesus Christ and, really, the story of how He has entered into each of our stories and brought us through.

THE GIFT THAT COSTS

> What, then, is joy? What, then, is sorrow?
> Time alone can decide between them,
> When the immediate poignant happening
> lengthens out to continuous wearisome suffering,
> when the laboured creeping moments of daylight
> slowly uncover the fullness of our disaster,
> sorrow's unmistakable features.[2]
>
> —Dietrich Bonhoeffer

Our journey began with our oldest son, Aaron. We never envisioned the grief we would someday endure and the grief we are still dealing with in his untimely death in 2011.

After our marriage, we were told the possibility of having children might not be a reality due to a medical problem I was having. We prayed, trusting God for whatever His Will might be. How thankful we were that I was able to conceive and our first son was born. He was a gift from God, a treasure, and yet unforeseen would be the greatest tests of our lives to seek God for answers about what this gift would cost us and our family.

By 1984, God had blessed us with four other children—two sons and two daughters.

Life was good. We loved the Lord, taught our children about Him, tried to live a godly life before them, served in our church, put them in a Christian school, and later homeschooled some.

I would venture to say, while we were and still are and always will be imperfect vessels, we were sold out to the Lord.

I say this because over the years, the message conveyed to me at times was that if our children rebelled or went astray, there had to be some defect in our lives, some reason, some lack of something to cause this. So guilt was added to the burden we already carried. Should we share or just keep it to ourselves?

What do you say for instance in a prayer meeting when you don't even understand yourself what is happening. Is it rebellion causing the bad behavior? All you know is your son's life is becoming increasingly more difficult. How do you voice your prayer request? There are others out there with more serious problems, or maybe this is just a common teenage scenario, so, many times one just keeps silent.

Many families I have spoken with over the years have been surprised when their loved one begins to show signs of some type of mood disorder. This is especially true when it involves the teenage years, which are already fraught with changes.

How hard to filter out just puberty issues from mental issues? In a home with children, there are always things that have to be dealt with, and in a loving home, who is looking for signs of some type of psychological disorder? We certainly weren't.

3

THE GIFT OF PEACE

> I called on your name, O LORD,
> from the depths of the pit; you heard my plea.
> —Lamentation 3:55–56 (ESV)

Our firstborn son, Aaron, died, August 18, 2011. My husband Dwight and I had not spoken to him in a couple of days. Aaron, for a number of years, had suffered with varying gastrointestinal ailments and also, in recent years, a back injury that seemed to be worsening. He was taking a number of prescribed pain medications and also those for anxiety and depression.

When Dwight drove to his home to check on him, he did not come to the door. Dwight went around to the bedroom window and, seeing him in his bed, called to him but got no response. Breaking the window and crawling in, he could see that Aaron had died. In disbelief and shock, Dwight knew he had to call 911—and me.

When the call came on that early morning, I had no idea of what words I would hear, and I was totally unprepared. I remember falling to the floor in anguish, crying out to God that this could not be real. It could not end this way. I screamed, I sobbed, and I felt the worst pain I had ever encountered.

I felt like the prophet in Jeremiah 8:18 (ESV). "My joy is gone; grief is upon me, my heart is sick within me." I cried so hard, my heart within me felt as if a knife were plunged into its inner chambers.

Our firstborn boy, our grown-man son, our beloved son who had challenged our faith in God and pulled us into a world we never knew existed, our prayed-for son, our brilliant son—now he was dead. I could not absorb the harsh reality.

Dwight could not be there with me, as he had to wait for the medical examiner. As I gasped for air, I found it difficult to breathe. My world seemed to be caving in. I lay on the floor and poured out my hurting heart to the Lord, and I knew that I would continue to cling to the Lord, even when all my hopes and prayers felt destroyed at that moment.

The Lord did not feel close to me, but He felt far away. I felt suspended in my pain. I felt so alone, flailing about like one drowning, yet I know now the Lord was there, waiting for the struggling to cease so He could pull me up out of the waves of despair.

I felt like Jonah in the belly of the fish—"For you cast me into the deep, into the heart of the seas, and the flood surrounded me, all your waves and billows passed over me" (Jonah 2:3, ESV). But at that time, I didn't get it. I cried out to Him, please, please let this be a dream. And it was. A heart-wrenching nightmare from which I would not escape.

I knew that I had to call family and let them know. I could barely speak; I sounded incoherent. As I had to call each one, it was agonizing. Soon our son Adam arrived. It was decided he needed to go be with Dwight, who was still waiting for Aaron's body to be removed.

What kind of a nightmare was my husband experiencing after finding Aaron's body? How did Aaron die? I hurt so bad that I could not even imagine what he was going through.

I do know that, at some very early point, I began to feel very detached, as in a dream. I could make plans, carry on a dialogue, and if at any moment, I began to think about what happened, I would simply switch to "off." I had prayed for that, asking the Lord to make a way of escape (1 Corinthians 10:13).

I would like to interject here that even in deep sorrow, Satan will be actively tempting to despair, but God promises we will be able to "endure" this temptation and urges us not give up.

I can look back now and see that God was giving me His Peace, His strength, and I was being carried along by His power.

"The Lord is near to the brokenhearted, and saves the crushed in spirit" (Psalm 34:18, ESV).

Our home became filled with family, friends, and those dear ones from our church. It was comforting, and it was a blessing.

Our children who lived out of state also began arriving. Each time was a new wave of weeping and recounting. Those who have traveled this road of grief know about the endless decisions that have to be made and the deadening effect it has on one's mind. In many ways, it was a welcome distraction from the pain

But now came the reality check—funeral arrangements. Only those who have had to bury a child know what that is like.

In the book *Lament for a Son*, the father of Eric Wolterstorff writes,

> What is it that makes the death of a child so indescribably painful? I buried my father and that was hard. But nothing at all like this. One expects to bury one's parents; one doesn't expect—not in our day and age—to bury one's children. The burial of one's child is a wrenching alteration of expectations.[3]

Added to our grief came the shock that due to decomposition of Aaron's body, there could be no embalming, no open casket. The horrifying thought of Aaron being dead and us not finding him earlier froze my thoughts into a total blackout.

My emotions were raw yet somehow cauterized. I could barely take in all the sterile facts I was listening to, yet I silently cried out to the Lord for his grace as we selected a casket and did the next thing.

"My heart throbs; my strength fails me, and the light of my eyes—it also has gone from me" (Psalm 38:10, ESV).

I understand now, as I reflect back on that dreadful time, the peace that passes all understanding. That it is given at the moment of greatest grief. It allows the mind to go into a hiding place—a numbing, surreal comfort zone.

"You are my hiding place and my shield; I hope in your word" (Psalm 119:114, ESV).

4

THE GIFT OF CLOSURE

> You are my hiding place and my shield;
> I hope in your word.
>
> —Psalm 119:114 (ESV)

We had to go to the house where Aaron lived. We wanted to find his address book to notify his friends. Something in me wanted to be there.

Some of the family felt like it would be too much for me and that I maybe shouldn't go. But I wanted to; something in me wanted some kind of closure or just to be there for reasons I could not explain.

The home he lived in was the home I grew up in. There were happy memories there. Those of us who went that day were not certain how it would be. The bed in which he had died had to have the mattress and box springs removed and disposed of.

I know we all were in some type of shock. We did what had to be done methodically. We found his journals, which was so much a part of who he was. How thankful we are to have them.

Aaron was an avid reader and writer. He had saved nearly every letter and paper from school and college.

Let me say here that this story would never have been possible, except due to the fact that he had written his thoughts, stories, poems, and hurts down on paper.

His struggles, I believe, are the cry of many today who are disabled in their minds. Did God not allow our son this outlet perhaps to help others?

Did I ever imagine that this intelligent, talented son would die so young or have so much sorrow in his life? He had so much to offer, so many gifts.

As we made funeral arrangements, I found myself participating as a spectator, someone wooden, cold. There were things such as the music. Aaron loved the music of Keith Green, so songs were selected and put together by our son Jeremy. Information had to be given.

At this point we still did not know the cause of death, but we knew it was accidental. Later on this was proven by an autopsy. It was due to an interaction of pain medication, an internal hemorrhage due to his bleeding ulcers. Why was Aaron prescribed so many drugs without monitoring their interaction?

According to the US Centers for Disease Control and Prevention, one person dies from a drug overdose every nineteen minutes. About 28,754 Americans died after accidentally overdosing on legal or illegal drugs in 2009. According to the CDC, about half of those deaths involved prescription painkillers.

As we gathered what to share, we, at that point, had not gone through all of the many journals of his. I regret this, as his writings were wonderful. But who is prepared for such a time as this? So only a few of his writings were read since there was no time.

Later, as I began to read his writings, I found what Aaron had written when younger, wishing we could have shared it at the funeral.

This was written in his early teens, when life was "normal."

> I have a tremendous, great thing to say. Before, I had things that I always wondered if were more than my love for God. I mean like, well, there were just things I would say I love God over them, but I never really knew it.
>
> Then last night I realized God was really my God. I mean, I want Him more than anything. Now I must admit

> I do things against His will, but I know it's wrong, and I repent. I mean, I really have God up there. I know that is who I serve.

And then when he was older, he wrote a long essay that began,

> I see God as Love. It's very hard to describe this love except to say when you resent it, try to hurt it, or stand in its way, it will only forgive. Forgive time and time again.
>
> Forgive by not resenting back, not hurting or standing in your way, and not "pressing charges" for your crime done to it (to this love) because obviously you want this love but have been hurt.
>
> And I have come to conclude also that God has made man in His image, meaning we possess an internal spirit or mind that under normal circumstances can communicate with God as a son to a father.

As I continue to sort through Aaron's journals, I realize that in many ways I never knew him. He was deep and yet put on a different mask many times. Did he ever really know himself?

5

THE GIFT OF MERCY

> You have kept count of my tossings, put my tears in your bottle. Are they not in your book?
> —Psalm 56:8 (ESV)

The funeral was held at our church. I felt detached and was able, because of that detachment, to remain very calm, and I remember as we and our family members walked down the hall into the auditorium, thinking how like this was a wedding—people rising as we made our way to the front of the church—but it was totally the opposite. It was not a time of elation, but of sadness.

All the clichés in the world about death mean little when it is your child you are burying. This was an abrupt separation—no sweet good-byes, just stark reality.

I knew and believed every word of God to be true, but the fact is, death is still an enemy, and nothing can change that. Knowing I would see Aaron again gives hope for the future, but one must walk this road of grief in the present moment.

I do appreciate so much those who reached out to us before and after the funeral. What would we have done without these dear ones?

But I knew, as I sat in the pew, that life for me would be different, and it was going to hurt. I awoke every single morning with such pain. As the realization would hover over me, I felt I could not function. I would cry out to the Lord, and each morning His grace and mercy washed over me, and I did the next thing.

"My soul melts away for sorrow; strengthen me according to your word!" (Psalm 119:28, ESV).

As I write this, almost two years later, has the pain eased some? It appears so, but, no, the feelings are just below the surface, hidden from view.

I miss my son more now than then. Why? Because the shock and detachment that were my shield are now gone. I miss the Aaron whom God brought into our lives.

This poem, which came flooding into my heart two years after Aaron's death, has helped me in sharing with others how one truly feels.

We try to take a small trip to the mountains around the day he died to have a time of reflection. As I sat in the quiet rustic cabin, I wrote the following:

Two Years Ago, And Yet

Has the wound within my heart
torn, bleeding, begun to mend?
And has the pain of Aaron's dying
begun to lessen? Soften? Bend?
Does time really heal the hole that dwells
in heart and mind?
Does my smiling face belie sorrow
that's hidden well behind?
No to all these askings, for the hurt will
always be.
But yes to God's enabling, sustaining, overcoming, all
sufficient, joy-filled grace to me.

The journals and varied writings of our son are windows into the minds and hearts of many individuals who suffer as he did.

The Gift of a Creative Mind

> Rejoice, o young man, in your youth, and let your heart
> cheer you in the days of your youth. Walk in the ways of
> your heart and the sight of your eyes. But know that for all
> these things God will bring you into judgment.
>
> —Ecclesiastes 12:8 (ESV)

Aaron was just a typical boy, loving to pull pranks on his younger brothers. He could be challenging at times because of his insatiable curiosity. He was a born leader, able to get his friends to do his chores for him, thinking they were privileged to do so. He did everything early in his life—walking, talking—and was able to write plays, movies and, using an 8 mm camera, have a cast of characters acting out his scripts.

Here's a poem written when he was young and so full of life:

> Flying
> Wouldn't it be jolly
> To fly with outstretched arms
> Flying, flying, flying
> Across the cotton through the skies
> Flying, flying, faster and fast
> Faster than sound, light, and laughter
> Flying, flying, faster than time alone
> But you say you can't do this?

> You're wrong! Your words are lies!
> When you've a goal to reach or try
> Don't give up, but aim to fly
> to that goal you reach,
> Standing tall, proud, and high.

Why did all that creativity at some point in his life turn in the wrong direction? When he was thirteen, late one night he became frightened. He said that he felt he was not a Christian, that demons were in the room with him. After praying with him, talking with him, he prayed, asking God to save him if he was not a Christian. Yet now, as I ponder that night, were there signs there or just godly fear or something dark and sinister?

To all outward appearances, Aaron seemed to be so happy. He had so many poems about his love for Christ.

> O Lord Jesus Christ
>
> I don't want our love put on the shelf
> I want it to be there
> I want it to be fresh and pure
> I want no part in its enemy, my lustful self
> Lord, I don't want our love put on the shelf
> No more You, I on my own
> O God, what would I do without You
> If it was there, then what if it never came back
> The sick, lonely feeling, there forever
> O Lord, I don't want that to happen
> No, Lord
> I want our love in my heart
> Me and You
> I love You more than anything

Yet as Aaron moved through his teenage years, things did change for him, things that did put God's love on the shelf. His fascination with the human mind and how it functioned, for reasons known only to him, caused him to experiment with drugs. He told us years later that it was curiosity that started the snowball effect, until it grew into an avalanche, suffocating him.

As I read Aaron's writings I see a struggle going on, a struggle he kept hidden. At age sixteen, again he wrote this:

April 25, 1984

> I have a problem. It is my witness. First of all, the problem itself is being a witness at work. I used to stand firm in my faith and all, but that was when I worked with ———. Now we have a lot more people at work. They aren't Christians and are into things like sex, beer, etc.
>
> It is hard for me to say, "I'm a Christian. I don't want anything to do with those things." What I want to do is say I'm a Christian, but still act "tough," and all, like I'm one of them. The root problem is one foot, my flesh, is too strong in my life and causes bondage in my life.
>
> What should I do? I know I'm supposed to be a witness. My job is to win those people over to the Lord, and I want to do that. But I want to be their friend. I want to love them and stand up for my faith, but I don't want them to think I'm a religious snob. Oh, Lord, help me with this matter.

At some point between the age of sixteen and seventeen, something changed in his thinking. I could speculate, but I never will we truly know the reason why he would make the decision to experiment with drugs. In doing so, he opened his life to dark forces which only have one purpose—to destroy.

THE GIFT OF SEEKING TRUTH

> Lead me in your truth and teach me,
> for you are the God of my salvation;
> for you I wait all the day long.
> —Psalm 25:5 (ESV)

In July 1985, Aaron wrote in his notebook,

> On the sin list I made, a big problem is with my parents. I don't respect their decisions, I don't keep my mouth shut when they do something I don't like, I go sneaking behind their back, and it needs to be stopped.
> A Christian must build discipline into his life. I have built it into mine, but it must go further. Next time my parents speak, I must learn to obey. Another problem I have is pride. I think I know it all, that I have the answers. But I don't. I have a smirk around home that shows just that. I must deal with that and rid it of my life of it.

We, of course, noticed this bad behavior, but we didn't attribute it to anything except teen issues. We had five children, and many distractions, to say the least. Something was happening in our son's life, and we did not at first see it. Never did we entertain the possibility of drugs.

Aaron wrote this account in his journal much later in his life, as a grown man:

> The analogy of the body
>
> At age 16, I began to induce [he lists the steroids he was ingesting here] into the system. Basically, I decided to use my body as an experiment and incorporate data.

Where did Aaron get the steroids? We assume now that it was at a part-time job he had at a ballpark, but who knows? And later, he used other serious drugs.

Thus began for Aaron his so-called experiments, and for our family, heartache, perplexity, and grief.

In his junior year of his Christian high school, he was expelled. Aaron at first acted cocky about it, as if it didn't matter. Yet it did matter, and he wanted to go back. He had to finish the remaining year at a public school.

During this time, we questioned Aaron about his life and behavior. He seemed to have an attitude and tuned out what we said. Then he would be repentant and would seem to be truly sorry. The school was willing to let him return for his senior year, provided he fulfilled certain requirements.

He was eager to be reinstated and complied with the stipulations. A poem I found in his writings reveals the struggle.

> The school was a righteousness, living on a line
> When I came, I stayed there
> Obedient to the law, I tried my best, I needed a rest
> But I went on, but then the troubles began
> Life could of have run, but I stayed, oh, I stayed
> I took it with a smile

He said later in his life how glad he was that he finished school, but during that difficult time his heart was beginning to harden.

Aaron wrote an essay—not sure when he wrote it—but it was revealing and honest.

> I've always wanted to beat the system and have realized that the system can be beat just as easy as it was created. So many conflicts have arisen and can actually bring them to equal status. But for what? I've realized that all systems are designed for the specific reason of trying to insanely try and beat them.
>
> An example, your mother and father will not let you do anything on Friday night. Not one thing, and for no reason at all. And you get mad and decide to take that system and turn it upside down.
>
> So you make their life miserable like they did to you. And you succeed. But is that good? You lost. You let the flesh take over and do what it wanted to do.
>
> To beat the system means to realize every system that comes about is to try and goof you up. The only way you goof is sin. To beat it, you realize that the system can be designed to teach and build character and realize it was God's will for it to happen.

Aaron knew the truth. He knew and understood things beyond his physical age. Having a intelligent mind is an amazing thing, but knowing how to use it to God's glory and to accept and adapt to the real world of imperfect reality was his stumbling block.

After graduation from high school, he began to openly pull away from us. It was constant friction.

We sought the help of a trained counselor. He met with Aaron on a weekly basis, and also with us. There was really no change, no answers. It seemed to be just a matter of rebellion on his part.

We would spend time with Aaron, seeking to understand, asking why he seemed so unhappy. We told him repeatedly we loved him and wanted to help him. It was frustrating and puzzling.

He began to listen to heavy rock music, even after he himself saw the detrimental influence it had on a person's mind.

So many well-meaning friends tried to console us with the idea that this was just a time of transition from youth to adult and it would wash out.

8

THE GIFT OF PRAYER

> Be joyful in hope, patient in affliction,
> faithful in prayer.
>
> —Romans 12:12 (NIV)

How does a young Christian boy change into a person you hardly know anymore? I believe it has to do with choices. His choosing to experiment, to investigate into the dark forces of this world bought him more than he could ever imagine.

He lived to regret all of that, but not until the damage had been done to his mind and body.

The question we have before us now is, did drugs so alter his mind that he developed mental and emotional disorders, or was it already there, lurking in the closet of his life? Of course, we realize that drugs do chemically and physically damage the thinking process and can damage the body to the point of death.

We have given up (almost) the tormenting questions that have been asked a thousand times. There comes a point when there are no answers. It doesn't make any sense for a talented young man to choose to play with drugs. Yet today we see that is becoming too common.

All the time Aaron was living at home and attending a local junior college after graduation, he was taking various steroids, unknown to us. These caused him to develop anger issues and a duodenal ulcer, as he wrote in a later review of his life.

Incredible urge of irritability emerged, bad temper (due to steroid) and an irritation of the lining of duodenal area due to the "TEMPER" project, and plus the knowledge that adding extra testosterone to the body at that age could create beneficial products but must not be abused. A six-month period of steroid was abandoned.

As a result of Aaron's experiments, his body began to produce large amounts of stomach acid. This would follow him all his days and eventually lead to many physical ailments.

I remember this time of extreme stress in my life. Our youngest daughter was going through various surgeries to correct a condition she had been born with. We were concerned greatly for our son but were hoping that he would do well in college and that life would level off.

After junior college, Aaron began attending a fairly close Bible college. His attitude while there would fluctuate between enjoyment of new learning and that of challenging what he was being taught.

At times, he began to act like two different people. He could be so compassionate and understanding and then act in a most unloving manner. How many prayers were made for him, only heaven knows.

9

THE GIFT OF COUNTING IT JOY

> You know my reproach, and my shame and my dishonor; my foes are all known to you. Reproaches have broken my heart, so that I am in despair.
>
> —Psalm 69:19-20 (ESV)

Then in March, we received a phone call to bring us to our knees once more. Aaron had been arrested for supposedly selling drugs.

During that awful time, I had kept a journal of what had happened following the ordeal.

> What I feel is overwhelming to my soul. My heart is broken and numb. I prayed until one in the morning. I am in a long tunnel. It is black, except there is a light at the end. I am not alone, the Lord is there too, but I cannot see my way.

After we drove to the school, we found out what had happened. Aaron had some pain pills (prescribed for his back), and he said he didn't know you couldn't give them to someone else.

The someone else was a boy who was to serve thirty-five years unless he would help the FBI to locate drug dealing. It was called entrapment. He begged Aaron for some of his pills, saying he was in pain. Aaron offered to give him one, but he insisted on paying him. And thus the arrest was made. Ignorance of the law is no excuse.

Even now, as I write about this and read my journal, I am again filled with such grief. Our other children, grandparents, friends were suffering as well. But it is the parent that suffers most.

We were told to contact a bondwoman named Ruby. We went to the jail. We sat on wooden benches.

In my journal, I wrote, "I see another world, and now I am in it. Why, Lord, am I in this place of shame and disgrace? Where are You?"

The woman, Ruby, begins to talk. She is friendly. She does this all the time. Bonds people, are on call twenty-four hours a day. She tells me she had a call at one in the morning. Everyone knows her. A young husband is there also to bail his wife out. People are coming and going.

This is another world. And we are here looking out of place, or do we? The people here are kind to us. Ruby tells me she went through this with her son, and now he is fine. She says, "You have a long hard road ahead of you." She offers encouragement. I am ministered to in this unlikely place.

March 23

> Got up very early this morning. I feel so depressed. A friend had shared with me when this happened that we would be able to help others somewhere down the road because of our having suffered like this.
>
> "He comforts us in all our troubles so that we can comfort others. When others are troubled, we will be able to give them the same comfort God has given us" (2 Corinthians 1:4, NLT). That will be great, but where is the pilgrim that has gone ahead of us that can help us now?
>
> When this happened, I had said to the Lord that I could suffer with joy if it was for His name, but this was not that! This was degrading, full of shame. I don't like it!
>
> Before I could spit out the words, the Lord spoke to my heart through James 1:2–3 (NIV).

"Count it pure joy, my brothers, whenever you face trials of many kinds, because you know that the testing of your faith develops perseverance."

Lord, show me *how* to count this mess as pure joy and not to give up.

Later I had also written,

I don't want to do my work. I don't want to cook, or teach (home school), or anything.

I want time out for grief. But there is none. Life goes on. Dishes have to be washed, food prepared.

"How long must I take counsel in my soul and have sorrow in my heart all the day?" (Psalm 13:2, ESV).

By God's mercy, I was able to surrender my struggling.

May 15

It has been some since I last wrote in my journal. Sometime between last I wrote and now, a place of "rest," has occurred. How can I explain what has happened except to say, I have, in reality, given Aaron completely to the Lord. I am not anxious or upset any longer, no matter what happens.

At some point I crossed the line and gave my burden to my Father in heaven. The trial has been set for June 5. What happens is up to the Lord. I feel now a real peace in knowing whatever God has to do in Aaron's life is necessary and good. Also, what people think has at least now, at this point, ceased to be a struggle.

I am sorry for Aaron. However he arrived at his personal ideologies, I do not know. It still saddens me extremely, but I *cannot* change that. He is answerable to God. My prayer for him is a holy life of righteousness, that he might know the truth and be set free. I long for him to be set free. But I must trust the Lord to this work in his life.

As it turned out, the charges against Aaron were deferred. The nightmare was over, at least for awhile.

But the things I learned during that time were going to be severely tested, and I would never have imagined the grief ahead of us.

The Gift of Endurance

> May you be strengthened with all power,
> according to his glorious might,
> for all endurance and patience with joy...
> —Colossians 1:11 (ESV)

How do we truly learn to persevere if there were no battles? "To persist in pursuing something in spite of obstacles" is one definition" of that word, but I never envisioned that I would be in a world with a son having mental problems. Wanting to give up, not persist, would be a better description of how one feels in the heat of the battle.

In all truth, had I not experienced it, I would perhaps have the attitude I see now in many others—the attitude that if one would only "straighten up, get over it, think positive," all would be well.

Mental illness is an uncomfortable malady. People, especially family members, are embarrassed by the person many times. It can be and is draining on relationships.

The tendency is to shy away from those who are "weird." We tend to cover up, deny, or get angry or frustrated with that one who is acting out behavior we cannot understand.

Treating a disease that is understood or treatable gives one at least a handle, something tangible to hold on to. Mental illness, while understood to some degree and helped in various ways with medication, therapy, etc., is still so frightening and uncharted.

After the incident at the college, Aaron wrote us a letter, thanking us for helping him and standing by him.

I wanted to say so much to you when I got out of jail, but I was speechless. I am beginning to feel the love you have for me, and I feel so thankful to have parents like you.

I just regret it takes so much to get through to me. And I wish I could make you proud of me and not bring you down. But I have a hope God's will is being manifest. I feel like an intelligent human, but certain principles and simple human tasks sometimes are so blind to me.

I am so naive and stupid. It's just dawned on me that regardless of what I believe, whatever authority I am under, I must follow their rules to keep away conflict. Your patience and kindness, Dad, has been an inspiration. And I appreciate your compassion to me, Mom.

I hope I can begin to live life in a more positive manner and not keep creating chaos. It has dawned on me how my behavior affects so many people. I grow weary of falling in my own folly and feel a peace within towards this new realization. I am just sorry to regret it brings you down also. I love my family very much and feel proud of every member and have love for you all.

In Christ,
Aaron Smoot

If only this could have been the "happily ever after" ending we hoped for. Why could not all he said have been implemented into his life, and I would not be writing this book?

I found a poem in his writings—or a song. It was indicative of his inner struggle.

> Oh, Lord, there are nights
> I lay helplessly in bed
> Staring into space
> Not knowing what I read
> My Bible is open
> And yet I don't see what I need to know
> And what You want to show me
> The struggles I have

> I want to do it my way
> I want to keep on going
> Yea, and send You away
> Finally in brokenness
> In my frustration and failure
> I give it to You, Lord
> Take my sin and wash it away

Aaron was very repentant after the school incident, but then he began to drift into unacceptable behavior. What was happening in his mind? Why was he resisting all the right choices once again? He was unable to live at home, to abide by our standards, so he moved into an apartment after obtaining a job. He seemed angry and resentful, and we were so perplexed and groping for some solution.

It wasn't like we were doing nothing. We sought help from Christian sources and also went to a group called Tough Love that met and listened to other parents pour out their frustrations to the group. Were we too soft? Were we too strict?

We, at this point, perceived Aaron as in a state of rebellion, not grasping the full impact of the darker side of it all. You just keep on praying, hoping that surely this will pass and that all will be well.

The Gift of Loneliness

> O Joy that seekest me thru pain,
> I cannot close my heart to thee; I trace the rainbow thru
> the rain, and feel the promise is not vain
> That morn shall tearless be.
>
> —George Matheson

It was a horrible time, and I found few that I could relate our heartache to. People cared of course, and yet it seemed at times we were so alone. Why did we feel so isolated? Did our pain and perplexity, cause us to withdraw, to keep silent?

Why did I feel that I could not share my heart with other Christian friends? So many times I had heard, "Train up a child in the way he should go..." You know the rest. Somehow I feel this was an unspoken thought, that our training—or our lack of it—was the cause. I, of course, knew of other families that had problems, but it seemed to be something no one wanted to talk about or hear about. It was spoken of in quiet, hushed tones, as if admitting to having a problem child was not to be discussed. When you are hurting, and raw, you can wrongly perceive the responses of others. This time of loneliness was a time to turn to the Lord, and seek Him.

All I knew was that Aaron was "departing," and we did not know why. How could we, or anyone, get inside his head. We tried. God knows we tried. We were shut out. How can you help someone who won't communicate?

Aaron wrote his thoughts on paper but did not share them with us. He was always writing stories, and there was one he was working on to become a book, we found in his journals after his death.

He wrote,

> Draft of book, main theme
>
> About the life of a individual person, a boy who is living a very easygoing life. Everything is going right for him. Then, suddenly, there is a change. Things start happening, not-so-good actions take place, and the boy plunges into a world of fantasy to hide from reality or reality of what is happening.
>
> His characteristics are those of a person who is more of a leader than a follower. He always has talks with himself because deep within him, he consciously takes in all his surroundings, and with deep internal an such thoughts. Going into this world of fantasy, he begins to follow his affections of violence, depression, and morbid lifestyle. He begins to change. People see him as completely different.
>
> He goes into a state of trusting only himself. He begins to fill his mind with all things having to do with the lifestyle he wants to follow and duplicate it.

This was supposedly a story he intended to write about a fictitious boy, but how much of himself is the true character? He also wrote about this as he continued on with the plot.

> As a whole, take incidents and thoughts going inside my mind and, in story form, learn of their roots and settle them by understanding that the life we should live should not be messed up with fantasy.

Individuals that struggle with reality versus fantasy seem to be in some type of internal war zone in their minds. How many times, do they, like our son, vacillate between the two?

In an essay entitled "Sin Nature/Insanity," he wrote,

Now come in focus with fantasy. Fantasy is, in short, mental illness. I can hear you now. Wait a minute, you say, I've had a fantasy before. I've imagined things, and I was not mentally ill.

There is a line to be drawn. Dreaming and fantasizing are WORLDS APART. Dreaming is a hope process. "I *wish* I were rich." A man dreams of a better future, hopes for a future as nice as the future in his dreams. Fantasy, on the other hand, is the belief of being. "I *am* rich."

So why did Aaron allow himself to succumb? The very thing he wrote about was, in fact, to become a part of his life, as this poem he penned later reveals.

> I live a fantasy
> All day long
> A fantasy
> All day long
> I wonder
> When the time is come
> And I know that it's not like some
> Who Know
> About the world they live
> And it can't be true
> Cause I'm not there
> That's thoughtless
> And it's just not fair

The Gift of Darkness

> Let him who walks in darkness and has no light trust in the
> name of the Lord and rely on his God.
> —Isaiah 50:10 (ESV)

Aaron began to have severe gastrointestinal problems and suffer from depression. He was prescribed some medications and an antidepressant.

Since Aaron was not living at home, he began to call us in the middle of the night. He would call sobbing or yelling in anger. Many times we could not understand him. It was each time a gut-wrenching ordeal for us. Sleep would be snatched away, and then what? We would pray for him, take a deep breath, lean so hard into the Lord to find light in the darkness and keep trusting when all seemed hopeless.

I can say truthfully, that just as God spoke to Isaiah and said, "And I will give thee the treasures of darkness, and hidden riches of secret places, that thou mayest know that I, the Lord, am the God of Israel."(Isaiah 45:3, KJV)

I was learning in these trials, that even though we wrestle with spiritual forces of evil in the heavenly realm, that we may stand our ground, and find God giving us what we need to move forward , and discover riches of His grace.

We, at this stage, began to search for a safe place for him, but where? For those who have a loved one that needs intervention, this is not an easy task. Where are these places? What do people do to find help? We found ourselves searching, and the choices were limited.

In our state of Oklahoma, we have, "the second highest rate of adults with serious mental illness, and also any mental illness, in the nation, according to the Federal Substance Mental Health Services Administration."

According to Mike Brose, executive director of the nonprofit advocacy group Mental Health Association Oklahoma, that those with mental illness will, "continue to wait in long lines and, when in crises, seek care in emergency rooms, the most inefficient and expensive forms of treatment."[4]

We could not, for example, just check him in somewhere without his consent. And those in crisis generally don't want help. If they are in a position to harm someone physically, there are places one can call, and the individual taken by force. But in some cases, it comes too late, and harm incurs.

On one of these episodes, when Aaron was in deep depression we implored him to seek help. Aaron consented, and we took him to a crisis intervention center, as he was threatening suicide.

After spending three days there, he was released and was required to be under the care of a physician. In these places of intervention,the time one can be there is a limited time, usually three to six days. Then what does one do with their loved one? The problem is not "fixed", but we were thankful there were places that did exist like this. We did not know at that time that this would be something ongoing in his life.

How can I describe what this is like? I cannot even begin to imagine or to minimize Aaron's anxiety or confusion, but for me—for us—it was such a time of darkness. Did I pray? Did my husband? Did the grandparents? Yes, we prayed, fasted, read God's Word for promises, read books, asked questions, sought counselors, and probed into every resource.

I poured my heart out with pen and ink in those intense times.

When all around me,
Other lives seem so
Much more.
And a thousand griefs
Spread 'round me
Like the sand upon the shore.
Do I rejoice within
With a glad singing heart?
That other lives seem so large,
And mine so small a part.
Oh, Father, Forgive my pride
My selfish thoughts within
Not unto me, do I desire to want this
(For self in me always wants to sin)
Father, today, this next hour
Can I trust that Christ in me
Will think, speak, love, Joy, care
Be my Life triumphantly?

13

THE GIFT OF COMFORT

> This is my comfort in my affliction,
> that your promise gives me life.
> —Psalm 119:50 (ESV)

In the next few months, some welcome changes began. Aaron began to attend a major university and, as he always enjoyed learning, seemed to be leveling off. Always I would think at each crisis, that all would now be well and life would be calm.

I have been recently reading a book in which the author said many times we fail to see the person as they are, keep expecting them to be the way we think they should be. You find within yourself a hope an expectation that is not based on reality.

It was during this time in 1997 that Aaron met and then married his wife. How happy Aaron was. He told me many times that he hoped for many children. They began attending church with us. We were overjoyed, hopeful. On Mother's Day, I received a handmade card and poem from him. He felt it was corny, but I loved it, and the fact of his apparent happiness.

> To my dearest Mother
>
> Through thick, through thin
> Mother, you've been there for me, during my wrongful sin
> Through tried and true, when I've been blue
> You, Mother, were there strong, and true

Thank you for helping me through my darkest times.
"If you've done it unto the least of the brethren, you've done it to me"

Love, your firstborn son, Aaron

Those first years of their marriage were sweet but also bitter. Since Aaron was the breadwinner now, working part-time and attending school became too much.

Lacking only nine credit hours to graduate with a degree in psychology, he withdrew from college. It proved to be a terrible mistake. Aaron was gifted in his ability to process information, but the only work he could find without a degree was not adequate. Over time, the financial stresses led to marital difficulties. Thus began for him—and for us—more heartache.

There were many situations in their marriage that caused conflict, many trials that would take them further apart. Aaron had always suffered from anxiety, even when quite young. Now, with all the stresses in his life, it became worse.

He had written about this in his journal.

> The main problem I suffer from is anxiety around people. For some reason, I fear them. Sometimes one would think I'm just fine, usually this is when I am around someone I am comfortable with. I enjoy being around people in groups, but when I'm with them one-on-one, I begin to feel anxious.
>
> Picture a boy running in the darkness. He is in the woods, and a bear is chasing him. He is all alone and is in much fear. He finally manages to make it up a steep ledge in which the bear cannot get to him. All night he is in a state of unrest. He was experiencing a natural reaction to extreme danger known as fight or flight.
>
> In turn, the human being also deals with internal threats and dangers he is never consciously aware of. The accompanying emotion's response is one of anxiety. Man seeks to avoid anxiety in every way. It can bring people under normal situations to feel as if they are being chased or like watching a loved one be murdered. It is very difficult for the

normal person to understand the pain these people, who are anxious, are going through.

He struggled to find work and became interested in working with the handicapped. He was able to get some certification and began working at a local nursing establishment.

It seemed to meet a need in his life to be of service. Aaron could be very tender and compassionate, and many times it caused him to get involved with individuals who were detrimental to his life.

He began to notice at his job that during after hours, some of the staff were mistreating some of the patients. He confronted the person in charge and was told if he knew what was good for him, he would "keep his mouth shut." He didn't and told them he would report them. The next day he was fired.

I recall Aaron calling me and telling me about this. He was angry. He felt that God had let him down. He felt that his job was meant to be, and now, instead of wrong being exposed and made right, evil had triumphed. I told him there must be some reason that God had for him being fired, but he was bitter and unreasonable.

In the weeks following, it was broadcast on evening news that the very same nursing home was being shut down due to misconduct and other allegations. I hurriedly called Aaron to tell him the news. I expected him to see God's hand in protecting him from being linked to the negligent employees, but his response was the same.

He began to feel that life was against him and that since God created life, then God must be responsible. He began to argue, dispute, challenge all the values he held dear. He began to blame others and, most of all, us.

14

THE GIFT OF WEAKNESS

> My grace is sufficient for you,
> for my power is made perfect in weakness.
> —2 Corinthians 12:9 (ESV)

In his journals, after his death, I found letters he wrote but never mailed.

> Parents,
> How did I become this joke? I know, yet I can't believe the humans' capacity to believe in it. Therefore I am coward. I am the man that cannot do that which I should do and want to do.
> Life is humility. It's a chemical reaction. Too much pride to destruct. I'll never send this. What I wish to write to you about is what is on my mind, yet no one is available. Will you SEE? How can you have the tools, the dedication, yet cannot comprehend the truth on a NOW basis. I don't get it.

The fact was, we did not get it. Aaron could be brilliant and then totally off the wall. We were always on pins and needles so much of the time. Aaron would imagine things that would be blown out of proportion.

In the next months, Aaron seemed to be getting worse. Losing his job and then having difficulty finding another led to great depression.

Once again, it climaxed in having to check himself in at a crisis center.

After this incident, it was decided he would be admitted into a psychiatric hospital for a week's stay

Now came the search for a mental facility that we hoped would utilize Christian principles. This had to be done fairly soon, which made it more difficult. Since my husband, an electrical engineer, was working, the task fell to me.

I was still homeschooling two teens at home, and I was committed to the daily disciplines and challenges in regard to that, so time was not something I had a lot of. Weakness? Yes, I knew about that, and I knew that if anything ever got done, it would require more than my best intentions. It would require God's strength.

Our weakness, placed in the hands of God, not only transforms us but sustains us in the battle.

As phone calls were made, I discovered what I already had somewhat learned—that finding adequate mental health assistance is a slippery slope.

Maybe one just assumes there will be a place available or that they can find help when needed. The reality is, many times, if a place is found, then there may not be a bed available, only a waiting list.

How many families struggle as we did in the maze of seeking help? Our son was not helpless but fully aware of his need, yet feared turning over the control of his life to others.

In our day of increasing mental problems, there sadly exists a shortage of answers to this dilemma. Here in our state, a sixty-bed facility recently has ceased to be operative.

In Aaron's case, a Christian-based psychiatric hospital was found. It was about two hours away. The cost for five days would be expensive since this was private, not state-run. We were more than willing to foot the bill in the hope he would receive help.

But what about those who cannot afford to do this? We certainly weren't rich, but we managed. Having access to get a loved one help in times of crisis should be more clearly defined, instead of the searching for what to do.

Senator Creigh Deeds, Virginia, is, in fact, working on new legislation in his state to improve mental care. His son Gus, twenty-four, in November of 2013, was in crisis and only detained for six hours. After being sent home, the senator was stabbed repeatedly by his son and taken by ambulance to the hospital, and tragically, while the senator was receiving medical attention, his son Gus took his own life. What was needed was a safe place for Gus, not to have him placed back into the home.[5]

15

THE GIFT OF HOPE

Now, Lord what wait I for? My hope is in thee.
—Psalm 39:7 (KJV)

As we drove to the hospital with Aaron, it was with heavy but hopeful hearts. Wondering if this was the right thing to do, what God wants us to do, wondering if there would be good changes and praying for a miracle.

So we left our son there that day. It was springtime; the year was 2000. We left him, driving home with a lump in our throat and a prayer in our hearts.

Aaron, of course, kept a journal while there. As I read it now, it is with tears and sadness. He was so despondent over his marriage and wanted for it to be solid. The things he wrote were touching, yet his marital relationship was very troubling. Aaron did agree that he was having some kind of mental issues and addictive behavior. This was an improvement, as he usually denied it.

He knew a lot about psychology after having studied it for his degree and also because of his fascination with the behavior of the mind. He had written in his journal that his diagnosis of himself was bipolar, nonmanic type (one that battles depression and anger for a while and then becomes a normal person, able to handle responsibility—his definition). However, the doctors concluded that they believed he was manic-depressive.

As we drove back to bring Aaron home, we were so hopeful for some sign of improvement. However, this was not to be. Aaron still seemed the same, only now he had a "label" attached to him—bipolar or manic-depressive. He was given new medications to help him.

It was a dismal time, and yet in the times of intensity in the storms of life, we can find comfort in the Lord. I wrote this:

> A storm is raging in the morning dark
> A storm is raging in my heart!
> The storm cries out with light and sound,
> Within my soul, my heart is bound
> With bolts of deepest pain I weep
> To You, I give this grief to keep
> Master the waves within my soul
> And bring Your peace and make me whole.

A letter written to a doctor concerning his medication put in words some of his ordeal after this.

> I, Aaron Smoot, used to battle panic attacks, nervous tension, irritability, and horrible gastric disturbance. Even taking 80 mg of Prilosec, I had to have some sort of short-acting benzodiazepine (Xanax, Serax).
>
> Problem: After a while, that began to defeat the purpose, and the physiologic addiction began to bring the same symptoms back.
>
> During this time, during a cold, I discovered after taking Tussin DM, 250 mg, all symptoms went away. In fact the strangest things occurred. I was able to stop the Xanax and Prilosec. Suddenly, I had no withdrawal, no nervous, panicky feeling, and no heartburn! I thought I had found a miracle drug.
>
> As time went on, I began to develop ataxia and slurred words and hallucinations. Then I began to feel manic and started to exhibit strange behavior. I began to develop a passive personality, being overly friendly, and then one night I heard an audible hallucination. I realized I had gone too far.
>
> I hospitalized myself at a rehab in ——, and they said I was acting exactly like a manic-depressive having a manic

phase. They said it may not be the DM. I knew it was, so I agreed to see a doctor, and for seven months, I did not take any medicine at all except for one Xanax a day for nervousness.

The doctor I saw diagnosed me as NOT having manic-depression. He took me off Xanax, and I took Pepcid AC only. I'm not suicidal. I'm not manic. I am an alert, intelligent person who made a mistake and have learned my lesson. I would like to continue the —— until I can overcome my nervousness and the —— to help me sleep at night.

Thank you, Aaron Smoot

Aaron had high hopes for his marriage, but as time went on, it only worsened. There were many problems in both of their lives. Many were in the extreme category. We were only the onlookers, trying to help any way we could but unable to intervene.

"I say to God my rock, why do I go mourning because of the oppression of the enemy. Why are you cast down, o my soul, and why are you in turmoil within me? Hope in God, for I shall again praise Him, my salvation and my God" (Psalm 42:9 and 11, ESV).

He became extremely fearful. His world was falling apart, and we found ourselves once again being sucked into the black hole with him.

Aaron had sent a letter to me, and I responded back.

> Dear Aaron,
> God has not given us a spirit of fear, but of power, love, and of a sound mind. (1 Tim. 1:7.)
>
> We love you. You are of great worth—both to us, to others, and especially to the Lord. Remember, in your letter, you once said, "I have a hope God's will is being manifest"? Don't forget that, no matter how awful things seem. Remember you said you want peace? You mentioned authority. You are right about obeying it. But realize there is no authority that is put there or allowed there, except by God's allowing it.

Whatever happens to you, you are not alone. I awoke early this morning with a hurting stomach. It was like I was feeling your pain. All of us are suffering because all of us love you, and let's face it, love suffers long.

Love you, Mom

16

THE GIFT OF REFINING

> For you, O God, have tested us;
> you have tried us as silver is tried.
>
> —Psalm 66:10 (ESV)

In the turbulent years of their marriage, Aaron's wife filed for divorce. It was a time fraught with raw and intense emotions. What was hoped for was now crushed and shattered. Divorce tears apart and leaves many open wounds.

I've often wondered about myself. Thrown into the many situations due to our son, would I have had empathy for those hurting parents as I do now, or would I have had just a critical view, as if I were above that?

Many dark and sinister days lay ahead for us. But we did not know it. I'm amazed at the grace God gives. We go through the days, even if we may crawl, but God is helping us in ways we don't even notice at the time.

We had weddings, births, and celebrations, even in the midst of sorrow. How true in Jeremiah 31:25 (ESV), "For I will satisfy the weary soul, and every languishing soul, I will replenish." God was kind to give us joy-filled days.

My mother, whom Aaron was living with, began to show signs of dementia. Soon it became apparent that she needed more care. We moved her into our home, to become her caregivers for the next eight years. This would become another chapter in my life of learning servanthood, and how little I knew about it. It was so easy to sing of it in church, but in the daily grind, one finds out its true meaning.

Over the next few years, Aaron would work at various jobs. His health problems began to increase. Since he had no insurance, it was difficult. We helped him as we were able. My mother's health became worse.

It was a struggle for me to watch her go downhill, and to see Aaron in such a state of distress made it more so. It seemed my mother's mind, and my son's, were in the grip of some force that was, at times, lashing out at those who loved them most.

There would be days when my mom would fall and injure herself, and we spent many times at the ER.

I would be so weary after such an ordeal, only to come home and receive a phone call from Aaron, who would be in either anger or tears over what he believed would be some new injustice. We knew Aaron needed more than we could give.

It seemed, many times, I could not bear all the pain. Only those who are or have been caregivers can relate. After helping my mother, seeing her acting out behavior that would be so out of character for her, I would go into my closet and lift my hands to God, telling him I just could not take it anymore and cry bitterly.

It is in the crucible, when we are being melted, refined, that we learn what dependence on God really means. "My eye grows dim through sorrow. Every day I call upon you, O Lord, I spread out my hands to you" (Psalm 88:9, ESV).

Here is a poem I had written during that time, when I was struggling with my own inner conflicts:

> Of what am I full of, of late
> A heart overflowing with love or hate?
> Why have I let my soul become so narrow, so cold?
> Why have I allowed the enemy
> to gain a hold?
> Oh, Lord, I lift my soul to Thee
> Take back Thy hallowed place in me

It was, and is, so easy to fall prey to self-pity, even if it seems justifiable. I felt I had my hands full with caring for my mother's needs, and my family. Oh, why, Lord, I would ask, why cannot Aaron's life be free from torment? Why cannot my life be free from torment?

In the book *Turn My Mourning into Dancing* by Henri Nouwen, which has been of tremendous help to me, he wrote about suffering:

> But suffering frequently teaches us a lesson about the incomprehensibility of God. Says God through Isaiah" For as the heavens are higher than the earth, so are my ways higher than your ways and my thoughts than your thoughts. (Isaiah 55:9)
>
> This is ultimately a freeing word. It invites us not to make God conform to our desires, not to try to fix the rules. For we cannot, even should we try, get God in our grip and think, *Finally, now I understand.* Rather, after all the turmoil or the long night is over, we come with an empty hand, one we stretch out to God.
>
> Our waiting on God, our asking questions about where he is taking us, can then cultivate in us a growing sensitivity to God's presence, as well as his absence. We learn to accept God's surprising ways and broken presence in our midst.
>
> Don't insist on knowing what comes next but trust that you are in the hand of God, who will guide your life.[6]

The next eight years were full of many ups and downs. Aaron continued to struggle, yet there were also many happy times. A letter he had written to his brother was a revealer of his many inner thoughts and emotions.

> I feel your grief over the death of a great friend of yours. I am sure you will turn the grief into another form of life energy. I pray you will see truth. All my life I have been in fear of telling you of subjects within life. You have charisma and are

> able to succeed in a world that I cannot. Pain and suffering are keys to the mystery of life.
>
> I could not stand to see you suffer. I would rather it be me. I have loved you through time, so much that it keeps me going. For my fondest memories of life were growing up with you always by my side. I took advantage of your charismatic ability and at one time became envious of you. I, in turn, lost your respect and friendship.
>
> I have been stripped of my authority and cannot even gain the trust of my own parents.

Aaron was referring to the failure on his part to maintain a job. He struggled to survive. He relied heavily on us. He was a good worker but had problems with understanding how people relate to one another in the workforce. He was too trusting, gullible. He didn't know how to be "cool" in today's world.

His ongoing health issues began to worsen. He developed ulcers and more gastric problems, due in part to the drug and alcohol abuse from earlier years.

The Gift of Solace

> For I am ready to fall,
> and my pain is ever before me.
>
> —Psalm 38:17 (esv)

One of the worse times that I would encounter was when Aaron was extremely depressed and experiencing explosive anger.

Most of these times, he would just have times of weeping and utter desolation. This time proved to be, however, heartrending and terrible beyond words.

My husband, with the other elders in our church, were in another state attending a conference. My mother was living with us still, as well as our daughters. Aaron called, and as I could barely understand what he was saying on the phone, I realized he was saying angry, hostile things, saying he would kill me.

No one can know what one experiences in a situation such as this. I felt like the life was draining out of my body. What should I do? In all probability, he was not even aware of what he was doing, but was he? I made the decision to take all of us to a motel.

I hated to call my husband and tell him, yet I felt he needed to know what had happened. As we spent the night away from home, I felt as if my heart was being torn from my being. Why was God allowing this? What were we to do? Where would this lead to? Questions that had no answers.

That night was forever ingrained in my mind as a night of horror. I was clinging to the Lord, even though my soul melted away for sorrow (Psalm 119:28).

C. S. Lewis, in his book *A Grief Observed*, spoke of questioning God.

> When I lay these questions before God I get no answer. But a rather special sort of "No answer." It is not the locked door. It is more like a silent, certainly not uncompassionate, gaze. As though He shook His head not in refusal but waiving the question. Like, "Peace, child; you don't understand."[7]

As it turned out, my husband flew back early. We felt terrified, uncertain of what to do. We decided to wait and see and fast and pray, and when we called Aaron and spoke about what he had said to me, he denied it really happened. He didn't even remember it.

Families that have a loved one in mental crisis are, many times, caught in this web of not knowing how far or to what extent that person will go to. This is your beloved child, not some stranger. You cannot even imagine such things happening.

I felt so emotionally wiped out that I longed for the Lord to wrap His arms around me and let me hide in Him. I found that solace there that only He could provide.

The ones whom we shared this with were also grieved. But people can only provide so much sympathy while the Lord is able to give the peace that is able to bring relief. How do we find this peace? We find it in the fire, in the pain, and we run to Jesus and fall into His waiting arms.

After this episode, things slowed down some. Maybe for Aaron came the realization that he had to make radical changes in his life. He began to seek help at a center that would administer medication to help someone who was bipolar.

One thing that always concerned him was the fact that if one did seek professional help and then tried to find a job, there would be questions on the application and then a background check, and once that information was on your chart, that you had some type of psychiatric intervention, finding work would be very difficult, as he had found.

Aaron also knew some individuals who purposely faked this so they could obtain medication and then sell it to others. He hated to have a label put on him, yet now he was becoming a broken man, not caring anymore.

In his writings he wrote this:

> There comes a time in a man's life when he begins to wonder what is real. What is man running toward? And why the hurry? I awaken each day, then a day goes by, then another, and without even lifting a hand, suddenly I find myself in trouble and in sorrow. Is that reasoning?
>
> I find myself needing to acquire advice, and yet my fellow man asks for a penny. When a man gets sick, does he make money? I fear to turn off the television. I have given it the opportunity to become a projection of safety. I pull my hair to unconsciously cry. My sanity is truly imbalanced. My stomach pains rage for truth and peace.

It seemed that we could do so little for our troubled son. Aaron had received counseling, both from Christian sources and secular. He had been to crisis centers and psychiatric hospitals. So many individuals like him were out there with mental illness, but they had no family to fall back on like Aaron did. How did they survive?

The Gift of Not Giving Up

> Knowing this, that the trying of
> your faith worketh patience.
>
> —James 1:3 (KJV)

In our church, we had experiences with a troubled young mother with progressing mental illness. Some of us tried to help. Over time, things became worse.

At one point, she became violent. People soon backed off. She drifted away, was institutionalized, and soon we lost contact. The Church—we, the Body—was unable to deal with her mental illness and help her. She frightened people, and the few that tried to help soon grew weary.

A dear friend of mine whose daughter still suffers from schizophrenia and at present lives in a facility has, for over forty years, had to deal with being the one for whom the burden rested.

As I write this, there are men and women I see out on the streets, homeless, drifting, many needing mental help, but unable to get any. My husband, who once a month goes to a local rescue mission to share God's Word, meets some of these individuals.

Many have families but were given up on. It is understandable. How perplexing, to try to reach out to the one you love, only to be lashed out at. Unlike a known illness, the sick mind is in a world all its own.

Somehow, though, it seems to me, that there is an assumption—wrong, of course—that Christians don't or shouldn't have mental issues. We have, as told in Scripture, the "mind of Christ," which, of course, is very true.

But we also have a fallen nature. We are subject to many ills, both in our bodies and in our minds. Can the mind get sick? Can a true believer in Christ, for example, succumb to depression?

If you have ever experienced this, you know it to be true. The reasons are endless—grief, illness, lack of adequate sleep, etc.

If by God's grace, we are able to overcome this time of darkness and become well again, we rejoice, yet some, like our son, don't move out of it but sink into a miry pit. Why? Who knows? Many times, even the person affected doesn't.

We see it happening. We are desperate to give help. But we find there are no easy answers. The friend I mentioned earlier said she never blamed herself for her daughter's actions but believed they were the result of her daughter's wrong choices. Nevertheless, she had to suffer the effects that this daughter's mental illness brought into her life.

She, like so many, trusted in God moment by moment, tear by tear, just as we were doing at this point in Aaron's life. How many times would I cry to the Lord for a miracle, a breath of fresh air to clear away the pain I felt?

Yet I would proceed with life, not sharing with many how it was. I do appreciate the ones who allowed me to share. Should I of been more vocal? Why did I feel that people wouldn't understand? Was I wrong to bottle up this grief?

Over the years I have heard from some who convey scorn and lack of empathy for those who are mentally ill. But do they consider the families, the hurting ones who are faced with this reality?

Those who are afflicted can be more than difficult. No one wants to be around them for very long. They say and do crazy things, embarrassing things, and sometimes medication that was intended to help does the opposite and makes them act and behave even stranger.

I find also puzzling the fact that some families I know of, who I would of loved to be able to bond with in our mutual difficulty, found it impossible to admit that their loved one was having any mental disturbance and avoided the subject entirely. Is it shame that keeps us locking our skeletons in the closet? Is the stigma of mental issues still back in the dark ages in the Christian world?

People who suffer with any type of mental disorder are real people. They are sons and daughters and husbands, wives, brothers, sisters, etc. They can be the dentist who works on your teeth or the mechanic repairing your car.

They take their medication, and all is well. They have learned how to survive, and no one even knows it. But for some, they don't take their medication. Maybe they have never found any that helps. Maybe they hear voices telling them strange things, like my friend's daughter, and they don't survive very well, and everyone knows it and says they're just crazy and laugh at them.

In another of our son's journals was this poignant writing of his confusion:

> Death abides upon my doorstep. Pride lives atop my roof, and the demons of confusion, hate, and superstition live within my soul because of my weakness and fear of this world. Yet I live godly, but in fear. I cast them out, yet they go live into the people I know. Search my heart, God, and I will spend my time singing praises of You.
>
> Maybe the time has come. I don't know. How can a man rejected from society, wondering if he left society, never understand the pain of loneliness? How can a man with such confidence of the truth be laid down and left to die? A fool can. Yet I knew and understood the fruits of our spirit that brought pain.
>
> I coveted the beautiful. I envied those who had the charisma to charm the crowd. I was jealous of those who ignored me and still yet still became successful. But my life, a life that was birthed into the love of Christ Jesus, would give

me futile endearment. I sunk into alcohol and dangerous drugs.

I temporarily lost my sanity. I became disturbed. Life left me. Friends and lovers condemned me. I suffered a terrible disease. Without a friend, without a visitor, without the wife and child of my love, I sunk into the house of mourning.

19

THE GIFT OF SURRENDER

> And yet, LORD you are our Father,
> we are the clay, and you are the potter…
> —Isaiah 64:8 (NLT)

And what about us? What about the family that is trying to understand, trying to cope, trying to pick up the broken shards and wreckage from this one who is in pain and causing pain.

I have witnessed denial, anger, resentment, shunning, and other reactions in our family. As stated before, a known disease has some map to show the outcome. Never knowing what to expect, what might be a trigger to set off some episode, is uncharted territory for those whose family member is mentally unstable.

There were times in the worst of it that I dreaded to answer the phone. I loved my son immensely, but I felt his hurt sucking the life from me. He would call and tell us of something in his day that was causing stress. It was selfishness on his part, and he was so blind to all but his own needs.

The Lord began to show me during this time that what I had learned in the school incident about surrendering my "fix it" attitude to Him needed rekindling.

I just wanted Aaron to be healed so that we all could live happily together. But I couldn't do this, and I must, for my own sake, let go somehow and trust God to orchestrate these lives, no matter what.

The lessons God had taught me were going to have to be implemented on a daily basis in my life, not just a one-time happening. I began to try to have a more realistic view of my life as it was, not how I wanted it to be. I was learning to open my hands to the difficult things in my life as blessings, not curses, and to be willing to accept that maybe things were not going to turn out as I hoped they would.

I began to study the life of King David and his son Absalom. David loved his son, even when his life was threatened and he had to flee. I could relate to that, after our own "fleeing" incident. In 2 Samuel 18:33, David has just learned of his son's death. "And the king was deeply moved and went up to the chamber over the gate and wept. And as he went, he said, O my son Absalom, my son, my son Absalom! Would I had died instead of you."

When David's army returned from their victorious battle, it was revealed to them that their king was deeply mourning Absalom's death, instead of acknowledging their victory. Joab comes to David with an indictment against him for his behavior.

> Then Joab came into the house to the king and said, "You have today covered with shame the faces of all your servants, who have this day saved your life and the life of your sons and daughters and the lives of your wives and your concubines, because you love those who hate you, and hate those who love you For you have made it clear today that commanders and servants are nothing to you, for today if Absalom were alive and all of us were dead today, then you would be pleased. (2 Sam. 19:5–6, ESV)

When we love someone, especially our child, we can be blind to a realistic evaluation of the true picture. We can become enablers, always hoping that soon they will change, failing to come to grips with what is the reality.

We feel sorry for them, we become nonobjective, and soon we are drowning in their brokenness.

God used Joab to confront David, and although in grief, he was able to rise above it and go forward.

As I pondered on this, I saw myself and all of us who love someone whose behavior is harmful. We keep hoping for some change just around the bend and live in denial of the true condition.

I was allowing my life to be focused on the dark side, instead of trusting God to be at work in ways I could not perceive.

20

The Gift of Acceptance

> The sacrifices of God are a broken spirit; a broken and contrite heart, O God, you will not despise.
> —Psalm 51:17 (ESV)

Did I *really* believe this? That God was working all together for good? I do know now, at this venture of my life, that, yes, He is. He is working all for His good and His glory. But that is now, and back then I couldn't or wouldn't see clearly. I was looking from my clouded perspective.

Aaron's divorce had a huge impact on his life—not only his mental state but, most notably, his overall health. He began to lose weight, developed IBS, and when helping a friend with moving furniture, fell and injured his back.

As I reflect backward into that time period, I can see God working in our son's life. Instead of anger, there was the beginning of humility. The physical pain was in some ways overriding the mental pain.

Also at this time was the worsening of my mother's dementia. It became necessary for someone to be with her at all times. I am thankful that we were able to care for her, even though I felt so helpless at times. I could not keep her from falling many times. I could be so close, and yet she would lose her balance, and down she would go. So many bruises, cuts, and stitches at the ER.

What was the Lord teaching me? Another lesson in the school of life—that I could not change, prevent, alter many of, if not all, of life's heartaches. What was the thread running through my life? To give thanks in *all* things, to count, reckon, and consider each difficult situation with trust in my Savior.

I remember so many times when I felt as if I were trying to "squeeze" out of myself a servant's heart. I questioned why God "allowed" dementia. It seemed that my life was wrapped around those whose minds were off track.

God, in his long-suffering, was patiently bringing me to the place again, showing me I had to always, always *not* look for what was needed to issue from me, but look away to Him—not just a casual glance but a trusting, penetrating look.

In my journal, I would pour out my desperate moments.

> July 6, 2007
>
> My mom needs sheets changed, she needs sponge bath, she needs bandage changed, she needs antibiotic on time, she needs her Ensures, she needs her nails clipped, she needs mental stimulation, she needs human touch and affection and compassion and patience, and she needs more than I can give. Father, help me. I depend on You.

Aaron was, at this time, undergoing tests. He was very ill. He began to speak of wanting to die. Many times our phone would awaken us in the middle of the night. Aaron would be sobbing so much that we would have to wait to fully understand his speech. Dwight or myself would listen, give whatever we could from Scripture, pray with him, and drop into bed weary and worn.

My mother's physical condition worsened every week. Hospice was called in. On September 15, 2007, my mom passed from this life. She lay barely breathing but said, "Jesus, I am waiting." Moments later she was with the Lord. How grateful I was to God that her suffering was finished and her rejoicing with Christ had begun. I thank the Lord for allowing me the privilege of caring for her, though I felt inadequate.

However, our caregiving for Aaron remained. Little did we know that in only four short years, our son's life on this earth would be no more. We had entertained the thought during the times when Aaron would talk about ending his life. But, as he would regain some composure, he would say, he would never do that to us.

I would not allow myself to really seriously consider that conjecture. It might be a fleeting thought, but for me personally, I rejected it.

I must be brutally honest here. There were times, for example, when Aaron would call and say horrible things, that he hated us, that he hated God. I felt anger at him, fed up with his tirades, and though I would never, under any circumstance, want any harm to come to him, at those intense times, I did wish for relief. And then he would call and say how terribly sorry he was for speaking to me like that. He said the pain in his body and mind caused him to lash out at those closest to him.

Those who are mentally sick can be very focused on their needs foremost. They have extreme self-obsession, of which they seem unaware.

We, the burden bearers, are expected to always rise to the occasion, to always be there and be patient, loving, good listeners. But there comes a time when one must hang up the phone, cannot always listen, and not always be there.

We had to get past being sorry for Aaron and come to grips with the choices he made when young—and the consequences. We were amateurs. We made mistakes. We enabled, not really understanding how or why or what to do.

In the earlier years, I stumbled around in the dark, searching for reasons, explanations, and answers to the utter frustration I felt.

Thinking that somehow I would at last have closure and that God would have Aaron help others by sharing his struggle and recovery. But now, yes now, all was changed.

I painfully had to admit to myself that I had no solid explanation or answers, that our son's life could possibly always be like this, and that I would either have to accept this way of life for us or grow bitter and blame God.

The son we prayed for, this precious but broken gift. Could I just say, "Thank you, God. I trust You in the days ahead, good or bad."

I believe that just as Isaiah recorded the words "Surely he hath borne our griefs and carried our sorrows" (Isaiah 53:4, ESV) that the Lord wanted me to allow Him to do this, to be able, in all difficulties, to walk in peace. I was learning to relinquish my frustration, to lean hard into him and not try to find a solution.

THE GIFT OF GRATEFULNESS

> Let me hear joy and gladness;
> let the bones that you have broken rejoice.
> —Psalm 51:8 (ESV)

In the next four years, Aaron began to assume more responsibility as he was able. He was taking medication for not only depression and anxiety but pain meds for his back and sleeping pills. He began to feel some better and began to read books again and take more interest in his appearance.

For some individuals, brushing one's teeth, bathing, etc., seems to be a struggle when the mind is off track. When his mind would clear, he was once again our loving son. Those moments were not taken for granted or thought to be permanent, but they were treasured.

A letter he wrote us was written in the last years of his life.

> Dear Parents,
>
> How can I express my love for you? Only my actions you observe are the actions of my love. Unwanting at times were actions I gave that did not want to be. When one loves someone, they tend to bite those hands. I have found the tendency for quite a while.
>
> It is a burden put upon my back I pray would disengage. I know as a youth, we did not get along about as much as we did get along. I held the bad within my heart for long periods of time. It clouded the times you were there with

open arms in time of my needs and blinded the wonderful times we had together.

Over time your examples have proved your positiveness of influence toward what you had on my life. The bitterness I had toward you is based on my mistakes and own ignorance. The things I've done, I despise and have suffered. I don't know how to live properly. Unaware of proper behaviorism, I blamed you. In reality, I must learn properly how to blame on my own terms.

Dear parents, I'm not perfect, but through time you both have forgiven me when I thought our time was over. One of my dreams, a very important dream, came true. The dream was to look forward to seeing you without feeling tremendous tension and guilt.

To call you on the phone and talk whenever is a miracle. You two mean the world to me. At one time, very long ago, I dreaded talking to you. I could not be myself. I envied others. Now that I can admit it, I can love you without squeamish tension. I apologize for such misfortune, and for depression, but I earned it by my lack of obedience. You have aided me in changing my life for the good. I hope you understand how much respect I have in my heart for both of you, my loving parents.

As Aaron's health worsened over the next few years, he seemed to become calmer and more receptive to a different lifestyle. His small income came from renting out one of the rooms in his home. He would work odd jobs from time to time at, but nothing that was permanent.

He would be doing so well mentally, and how we enjoyed those times with him, and then overnight, all would collapse into some type of trauma.

Were we now "conditioned" or more able to deal with the stress? Do years of struggle make you tougher or wiser? I can only speak for myself and say that each time, I would cry out to the Lord and reaffirm my trust in Him to carry me through, and God always gave what was needed most.

I realized in the battle times to ask some to pray. It seemed those who had or were also dealing with someone like Aaron could pray with understanding.

In the last years we did not really share much. Even some in our family had no patience or desire to hear about Aaron's problems. How thankful that

"I am overcome with joy because of your unfailing love, for you have seen my troubles, and you care about the anguish of my soul" (Psalm 31:7, NLT).

Aaron began to write us letters. Sometimes they were not rational, but always they were complex. Reading them, are they not the thoughts of many whose minds function on a different plane? This letter, however, was very clear and revealing.

> Okay, Mother, it is now 3:25, and I just got off the phone. I am learning word understanding and can hardly write because each pause or syllable has such an intuition in itself. Another letter I would have never mailed. But you said you like the letters. To me letters are of paramount importance. Writings and sayings give way to gravity. You see me in person. I do not know how to contrive. I act off of others. I feel at peace, yet what comes out is frustration. I have compassion, yet I act out in combustion. I have an instinct to analyze every angle, every gesture, movement of the eye.
>
> What is my occupation in this world? My mind is alive, yet the world wishes it to be dead. My flesh, many times, have numbed it to stop. I have become cowardly toward living, having no boldness to tell of my mind, to speak my mind's truth. I've allowed myself to be sunk, yet I cannot be sunk in!

Aaron wanted so badly to be understood. And we wanted so desperately to understand. Yet there was a barrier. He loved God but at times would turn against Him. Why is it that some wrestle with God all their lives?

22

THE GIFT OF COMPASSION

> It is of the Lord's mercies that we are not consumed,
> because his compassions fail not.
> They are new every morning:
> great is thy faithfulness.
>
> —Lamentations 3:22–23 (KJV)

William Cowper, a hymn writer who died in 1800 and suffered from ongoing mental illness, died in that condition unhappy. John Piper states, "You cannot persuade a depressed person that he is not reprobate if he is utterly persuaded that he is. But you can stand by him."[8]

In those times of late-night phone calls from Aaron, all we could do was "stand by him." But getting back to sleep was difficult. I had to remind myself most of the time that there were things I would never understand and that this was one of them. I was being taught by the Lord that it wasn't vital that I knew the answers but that it was vital that I knew my Savior.

I could love my son, even when he was unlovely. I could receive from God the strength to accept what could not be explained and still have joy. Why? Because God was my joy, and for so many years I thought getting things "fixed" in my life would supply that joy.

I can see myself in the apostle Peter. When Jesus began to tell the disciples of his forthcoming death, Peter took Him aside and began to rebuke Him, telling Him, "Far be it from you, Lord! This shall never happen to you" (Matthew 16:22, ESV).

In my case, I, too, thought that I shouldn't have to have these things happen to me. And the word that was given to Peter was a word for me. "But he turned and said to Peter, 'Get behind me Satan! You are a hindrance to me. For you are not setting your mind on the things of God but on the things of man.'" (Matthew 16:23).

For so many years, my focus was finding solutions instead of setting my mind on Christ. How many of us with troubled love ones focus on them so much and lose sight of the things of God? He alone is the solution to every imaginable dilemma we will ever encounter. Did I slow the process by denial? Were my eyes blinded by refusing to admit to myself that our family was dysfunctional?

In truth, in ourselves we are all dysfunctional. We are all sinners. If not for the imputed righteousness of Jesus Christ, we are all filthy rags. I believe my husband and myself had the false assumption that since we had prayed so much for this unborn child back then, that God would of course never give us a son who would cause grief.

God had been teaching me, in the years of caring for my mother, to be thankful for small things. Some days with her declining dementia would be days of clarity and more lighthearted times. How glad we were for those times.

Now, with Aaron, I could be thankful for the days when he could joke and have fun with the family. On the days that were not pleasant, I could still be thankful. Did I always do this? No, I admit it wasn't easy, but the wonderful grace of God helped me time and time again.

Aaron, in those last years, with declining health, seemed to have less depression. For so long the focus was his mental health, and we really never knew how ill he was becoming. We were just thankful that he was more settled and content than in previous years.

In the neighborhood where he lived were many homeless people, due to a shelter nearby that gave some assistance. His home was on their walking path, and Aaron made friends with some of them.

In a letter to his brother Jeremy, was this account, as only he could write this:

> I know all the homeless people by name and, quite so often, go visit their camp in the woods behind Conaco. It's like going into, well, you follow this path into a large grove of persimmon trees and start to see little campfires and homemade lean-tos and forts made of wood and cardboard.
>
> One guy may be playing a harmonica. Always at least two or three are passed out or sleeping. These guys know everything about the street—who died, jail stories, what's being built, who is panhandling, etc. I have given them clothing, food, and, ever so often, spare change. (Never give homeless people money, they will bug you for more.)

Aaron had a great sense of humor, and he also had a heart for the downtrodden. He knew all about a part of life that we knew little of. He had experienced so much of what these men perhaps had gone through in their lives—wrong choices, consequences, shame, and humiliation.

I, too, because of Aaron, now view those who are outcasts in a different light. How and why they are where they are, I'll never know. Somewhere they took a wrong turn. I wonder always about their families. Are they praying for their derelict son or daughter on the street corner holding up a sign?

I silently pray for them. God the Prodigal Father running to meet His wayward children when wasted lives turn in brokenness to true repentance. But for some, too many years of abuses have numbed the mind but, we know, not the heart. God knows.

As I look into the face of a panhandler standing in pouring rain, I must pray. My own heart has been crushed for my own child. I cannot be indifferent.

23

THE GIFT OF GUIDANCE

> Trust in the Lord with all your heart,
> and do not lean on your own understanding.
> In all your ways acknowledge him,
> and he will make straight your paths.
>
> —Proverbs 3:5–6 (ESV)

In 2010, his back pain was getting worse. The condition was a degenerative disk and sciatica. This once again brought on more depression. An antidepressant was prescribed. Aaron began to act like someone in a drugged state, with slurred speech. Once again the phone calls began, and the crying. Many times we would just sit with him after driving to his home. In my journal, I wrote this:

> Aaron calling all day long. Calling everyone. He fell, hit his face, is in a drugged state. Dwight and I tried to talk with him all day. Don't know what to do. Heartbreaking depression. How long will this go on? Aaron is probably taking too much of his pain medicine. What can we do? He needs help, but what?

This was on a Friday. On the next day, I was reading a health magazine, and inside was an advertisement about certain antidepressants that had extremely detrimental side effects, even causing one to become suicidal. The article was called, "The Marketing of Madness."[9]

There was an online video one could view It was the same drug our son was now taking, and the more I read, the more it sounded like Aaron's condition.

I called him and told him about the side effects, and he fortunately agreed to wean himself off of the pills. I know that God, in His mercy, once again had intervened and brought help when we needed it.

I began to do some research on the dangers of antidepressants. An article by Dr. Peter R. Breggin, MD, was helpful.

> On March 22 the FDA issued an extraordinary "Public Health Advisory" that cautioned about the risks associated with the whole new generation of anti-depressants including Prozac and its knock offs, Zoloft, Paxil, Luvox, Celexa, and Lexapro, as well as Welbutrin, Effexor, Serzone, and Remeron. The warning followed a public hearing where dozens of family members testified about suicide and violence committed by individuals taking these medications.[10]

Aaron's physical pain, as well as his mental pain, caused him to turn to drugs many times. And while I realize and appreciate the benefits, are we not too quick to want relief at the expense of something much worse?

Many times as Aaron would have a medical appointment at a clinic, he would receive yet another prescription for pain, or sleeping pills, or something for anxiety. Who is to monitor all these drugs? Many times he would forget he had already taken some and then would ingest more.

We struggled with ways to help. Perhaps he could move home? He did not want to do that. If I allow myself to look back and say what if or if only, I will descend into the pit of regret, which has nothing but misery there. I know, because I've been there, and it will devour. So I choose to focus on the facts that by God's grace, we did all we could do, and I rest in His peace.

After this episode, Aaron's mind seemed to clear, and once again life continued on. It was a roller coaster life with our son, and we had to accept that.

The Gift of Grace

> And after you have suffered a little while,
> the God of all grace, who has called you to
> his eternal glory in Christ, will himself restore, confirm,
> strengthen, and establish you.
> —1 Peter 5:10 (ESV)

In the last year of Aaron's life, someone he loved dearly paid him a visit. It was told to Aaron, of this one becoming a Christian. We rejoiced along with our son over this news. However, in the days ahead, the truth was that this individual was involved in a cult. Aaron, who was hoping for renewed friendship, now found himself in a difficult situation. Did he confront this one with the truth or just dodge the issue to keep the friendship?

He went and bought himself a newer version of the Bible and shared with this one the truth of God's Word. It was not easy, but, thankfully, he did it. The outcome was, this one walked away and would not receive the truth. He wrote in his journal of the grief and hurt he felt over the incident. But even though wounded, he was able to rise above it and move forward.

Aaron's health, which had, for a while, seemed to improve, began to worsen. The sciatica had caused so much pain, he could barely walk. He began using a cane. Unknown to us was just how serious also were the stomach ulcers he had. He had lost a great deal of weight, and we were so concerned.

He had, on numerous times, been to the ER. He was taking an assortment of prescription drugs. These included sleeping pills, painkillers, and anti-depressants. We somehow took it for granted that these were being monitored, and that Aaron was mentally cognitive enough to take them correctly.

But the truth was, he was not, and had been taking them sometimes twice in one day. We discovered this when at one point, his speech became slurred.

Here is the dilemma of those like ourselves, who love and care for those mentally unstable. We cannot force them to comply with what we deem best for them. And so we find ourselves like so many others, not really having the best answers. So many times I would just go outside and sit on my porch swing and weep, and pour out my helplessness to God. He was faithful every time to bring me his strength.

There were days when he would tell me he felt he was dying. This was not anything new. He had always talked of death when depressed, and I would try to cheer him up.

I could not—or would not—allow myself to go there. God was in control, and all would be well.

Just months before Aaron's death, something happened that we would never give much thought about, but now see more clearly. My husband's uncle had passed away, and we were to meet with family members about the grave plot allotments. As it was discussed, there was one space left, and we were asked for whom might it be given to? Since Aaron was the only single family member and since he had little income, it was designated for his future use.

As we walked around the cemetery, did I ever envision actually burying our son here? No, because it is the parents who go first. Even though Aaron had frail health, it did not cross my mind.

Another one of Aaron's writings that were in the notebooks he had saved was a very unusual one. I have no idea when it was written or why. When I found it, what I felt as I read it was such a surreal moment. He had written his own obituary.

Aaron Smoot died the other day at an unknown age. It was never found out as to the cause of death. The mysteries and secrets he pursued were never quite understood by the human race. His life was filled with an odd assortment of various guises, in which no one could ever tell what would be next. His accomplishments meant nothing, save for the fact that he only wanted the smile of God's face upon his life. He prayed that in spite of the stunts he pulled, that he would be remembered as a meek and gentle being.

I will never understand the complex workings of our son's thoughts, never know why he found reality so painful and why he would even experiment with his mind.

Do any of us truly comprehend the inner heart cry of another? "The heart knows its own bitterness, and no stranger shares its joys" (Proverbs 14:10, ESV).

I marvel at the many stories, articles, journal outpourings that Aaron wrote over the years of his life. He told me that several of his private journals had been destroyed at one point in his marriage and how grieved he was about it. I understand now. This was a way in which he could unload all the deep turmoil of his troubled life. How many, like our son, have many guises to hide the pain they feel?

Another one of Aaron's poems we found was so encouraging. When it was written, I do not know.

> As I walked down the road, I noticed in that deep blue sky, a new day. And as I walked down that long road, I chanced a breath of fresh air.
> Ah, yes, and it replenished my lungs with such appetite! And I glanced out. I looked into those magnificent skies and realized, hey! You're you. And I was filled with joy!
> I can be me.

> I don't have to put on a show. I don't have to explain, or predict. I don't have to plan out, or go against. I can just be me.
> Oh, and the joy. Yes, the urge to sing. And my spirit arose, and my troubles flew away.
> Look, I'm real! I'm different!
> I have a me inside, and it can be seen!
> Sure, they'll misunderstand
> Sure, they'll call me weird or strange
> Sure, I'll get hurt
> and mad
> Even make a few mistakes (can you multiply that please)
> But I am the one still walking. I'll smile and laugh for joy.
> ANGER
> It's only my fault, not theirs. For just to live is to realize it will come.
> And if faced with doom and loneliness, and it lurks inside me, as if hiding, afraid to show.
> Yet I smile
> And look forward to a new day.

Yet in all this, there are choices to be made. We all, at times, make wrong ones. The consequences that issue from them can be life changing. If we are a child of God, even if people may give up on us, God doesn't.

What a comfort to those of us who love someone who struggles with a broken life. The Lord is the mender of broken vessels, if one can only receive the grace that is given.

If not received, then God cannot be blamed for the cracks and shattered pieces in the outcome. We, too, the ones on the sidelines, can choose to allow the grace of God to so sustain us as we look on with holy trust.

For me, receiving from God the gift of our son, with all the emotional ups and downs, has taught me and still teaches me more than I could ever imagine.

When I hear of a family whose son or daughter has brought them grief, or a newscast about a crime committed, I hurt for the ones who have loved them, have perhaps tried to help them, but failed. I pray for them now, that they, like me, might have the peace that only God can supply and that they receive with open hands His marvelous grace.

Aaron's gift to me on Mother's Day was this card he made and illustrated with drawings of mountains and valleys so like his life. I'd like to think of him now, as he crosses this life into the next, finding rest from his struggles on earth, finding Jesus to be his greatest treasure.

Le Mysterie

Now I go to close the door
Forgetting time and to swim the shore
And then one day, I pray you'll find
The smoothest mystery, the only kind.
Then shall the dust return
To the earth as it was
And the spirit shall return unto God who gave it.
All we have is an Eternity waiting…I love you

25

THE PRICELESS GIFT

In closing, I would just like to tell of the greatest gift I have ever received. It is the Priceless Gift, the gift that God gave, the gift of his son, Jesus Christ.

> One will scarcely die for a righteous person—though perhaps for a good person one would dare even to die—but God shows his love for us in that while we were still sinners, Christ died for us.
>
> —Romans 5:7–8 (ESV)

All that God did for us, all the gifts he gave us in our times of suffering, was not because we were saints or sinners, but because of his mercy. We trusted in him, but sometimes we doubted.

We moved forward, but also fell backward.

Trusting in Christ for salvation is totally dependent also on his mercy. What joy there is to know that just as we could never have been the perfect parents to our son Aaron, we can never be good enough to earn eternal life.

Praise God that Jesus Christ was!

> For by grace you have been saved through faith. And this is not your own doing, it is the gift of God, not a result of works, so that no one may boast.
>
> —Ephesians 2:8–9 (ESV)

Postscript

In December of 2014, we received a phonecall from The Oklahoman newspaper. The gentleman informed us that our son, Aaron Smoot, was one of nine individuals who had died while in the care of one particular physician, and that his death was due to the prescribing practice of highly addictive drugs that were not monitored correctly.

This news came as a shock to me, yet as I wrote in the book, I had already voiced my suspicions about this but had no tangible proof. This doctor in 2012, had his state board medical license revoked and is no longer practicing.

The newspaper did a feature story on us and a video in an attempt to make the public aware of the growing number of deaths due to accidental drug overdose and the easy availability of prescription drugs with no accountability of the ones administering these powerful drugs.

The article went on to report that this clinic recently had another physician sentenced to prison for second degree murder for prescribing and contributing to the death of one man.

The article went on to say that last year, unintentional prescription drug overdose deaths in Oklahoma claimed more lives than automobile accidents.

The way our son was portrayed in the article was insensitive, and while he was taking a number of medications, he was not a known drug addict as implied. Even though the article took liberties with our statements, I trust that God will use this to work together for good, and that by God's grace, some may be helped by our story and Aaron's life.

Notes

1. Alcorn, Randy. "How God Uses Suffering for Our Sanctification." In If God Is Good. Colorado Springs: Multomah Books www.epm.org, 2009.
2. Bonhoeffer, Dietrich. "Sorrow and Joy." in The Martyred Christian. . Reprint, New York: Macmillan, 1983.
3. Wolterstorff, Nicholas. Lament For A Son. Grand Rapids: Wm. B. Eerdmans, 1987.
4. Cosgrove, Jaclyn. "It's a Feeling of Hopelessness, Loneliness, Unhappiness." The Oklahoman, July 22, 2014, Daily edition, sec. Front page
5. Blumm, K. C. "Sen. Creigh Deeds Talks About Stabbing, Son's Suicide." People.com (accessed January 1, 2013).
6. Nouwen, Henri. "From Holding Tight to Letting Go." in Turn My Mourning Into Dancing. Nashville: Thomas Nelson, 2001.
7. Lewis, C. S. "Chapter Four." in A Grief Observed. Reprint, New York: HarperCollins, 1994.
8. 8. Piper, John. "When the Darkness Does Not Lift." in When I Don't Desire God. Wheaton: Crossway Books, 2004.
9. 9. The Marketing of Madness. Film. The PepiTube
10. 10. Breggin, M .D., Peter R. "The Proven Dangers of Antidepressants." http://breggin.com/index2.php?option=com_content&task=view&id=1.(accessed January 1, 2014). Blumm, K. C. "Sen. Creigh Deeds Talks About Stabbing, Son's Suicide." People.com (accessed January 1, 2013).

2013, our children and their families

our three sons

1987, our five blessings

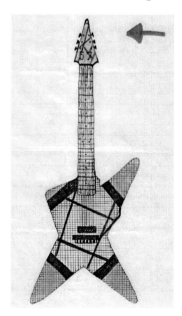

Aaron repeatedly drew guitar images in his journals

Aaron's drawing, perhaps of himself?

Aaron's graduation photo 1986

Challenging days

CPSIA information can be obtained at www.ICGtesting.com
Printed in the USA
LVOW10s1330090916

503941LV00023B/306/P